A TEMPLAR BOOK

First published in the UK in 2023 by Templar Books,
an imprint of Bonnier Books UK
4th Floor, Victoria House,
Bloomsbury Square, London WC1B 4DA
Owned by Bonnier Books
Sveavägen 56, Stockholm, Sweden
www.bonnierbooks.co.uk

This book was produced in partnership with the Royal Botanic Gardens, Kew
© The Board of Trustees of the Royal Botanic Gardens, Kew
(Kew logo TM the Royal Botanic Gardens, Kew)

Text copyright © 2023 by Emily Dodd
Illustration copyright © 2023 by Chorkung
Design copyright © 2023 by Templar Books

1 3 5 7 9 10 8 6 4 2

All rights reserved

ISBN 978-1-78741-808-0

This book was typeset in Catalina Clemente
The illustrations were created digitally

Edited by Ruth Symons
Designed by Nathalie Eyraud
Production Controller Ella Holden
Printed in China

Tell me about...
PLANTS

Written by
Emily Dodd

Illustrated by
Chorkung

Contents

Plants are Wonderful............. 8

Parts of a Plant.................... 10

Flowers 12

Fruit 14

Getting Planted..................... 16

Seeds 18

Drinking Water 20

Making Food 22

Organising Plants 24

Flowering Plants 26

Grasses 28
Trees & the Seasons 30
Types of Tree 32
Leaves 34
Defence 36
Plant Attack 38
Weird & Wonderful 40
Thank You, Plants! 42
Glossary 44

Plants are Wonderful!

They look good and smell great! They provide us with tasty treats like chocolate and strawberries. We use them to make paper and boats and furniture and bike tyres and even underwear — your cotton pants are made from plants!

Plants are living things. Like us, they need air, water, light and food to stay alive.

Yummy sun!

But plants don't buy their food in a shop and eat it off a plate like we do.

Instead, plants use sunlight to make food!

When plants make food, they also clean the air. They take pollution out of the air and they release a gas called oxygen.

Oxygen is the gas all living things need to survive – we breathe it. So life on Earth can only exist because of plants!

Did you know...?
Some plants are taller than skyscrapers. Some are smaller than a full stop.

There are poisonous plants, and animal-eating plants and plants that smell like poo!

There are more than 400,000 types of plant on planet Earth.

Parts of a Plant

Plants are made of parts that can look quite different to each other. This tree has a thick woody stem called a trunk. The buttercup growing beneath it has a thin bendy stem. But they are both still stems!

The stem carries water and goodness around the plant. It holds the whole plant up.

The roots anchor the plant and take in water and goodness from the soil.

Flowers

Flowers look nice and smell great for a reason. They want to attract insects. Insects help flowers make seeds, and seeds are really important because they are the beginning of tiny new plants!

Petals make smelly oil and a sugary juice called nectar. This makes them smell good to insects – and to us!

Colourful petals point insects to a sweet treat.

Petal

Yummy nectar!

Anther

Anthers are stalks with a sticky powder called pollen on them.

The bee accidentally brushes past the anther and pollen sticks to her fur.

The bee visits another flower, and some pollen comes off.

Stigma

When pollen touches the stigma, a tube grows down, taking the pollen to the ovary.

Ovary

The flower uses the pollen to make seeds. It does this by turning into a fruit!

Did you know...?
Pollen looks like a fine powder to us. But close up, the tiny grains are amazing shapes!

Lily

Sunflower

Nasturtium

Creatures that carry pollen between flowers are called pollinators. They include moths, mice, and even bats!

13

Fruit

Flowers turn into fruit. That's right, melons used to be flowers! When you hear the word fruit, you probably think of tasty apples, bananas and oranges. But there's more to fruit than what goes into a fruit bowl. Nuts, seed pods and pumpkins are fruit, too. Fruit is just the thing a flower changes into – it's a shape with seeds in it.

Peas are tasty round seeds that lie safe in a long flat fruit called a peapod.

A strawberry fruit has seeds on the outside of its body!

A horse chestnut fruit is green and spiky. It protects one big round seed called a conker.

Pomegranates are fruits full of seeds. Every seed has its own soft red coat.

The sycamore tree has a winged fruit. When it falls it twists like a helicopter.

A poppy flower turns into a fat, round seed pod with a hat. This fruit contains thousands of tiny black seeds!

Hazelnuts are fruits with one seed inside them. It's called a nut and it sits inside a hard nutshell.

Did you know...?
A nut is a hard fruit that doesn't fall open by itself.

Getting Planted

Plants need their seeds to grow into baby plants – their plant children! But first, a seed needs to leave its parent and reach the ground. There are many ways a seed can get planted in the ground including...

Hiding in tasty fruit, being eaten and... being pooped out!

Exploding through the air

Bird poo has goodness in it that helps plants to grow!

Rolling, rolling, rolling...

Floating in the sea and washing up on a beach

Seeds

Seeds are amazing! One tiny seed can grow into a big bushy plant. Inside a seed is a food store and the instructions to make every part of a new plant. This is how it happens...

A seed will grow when it is:
- dark enough
- wet enough
- warm enough
- the right season

1. Wake up
The seed lies in the dark earth. It needs water and the right conditions to wake up and start growing.

2. Bursting out
A root grows down and a shoot grows upwards. They know which way is up, even though it's dark and a seed can't see!

Yawn!

Shoot

Root

Plants are made of tiny building blocks called cells. A cell can copy itself and split in half to make two new cells. That's how a plant grows. The same thing happens with the cells in your body as you grow!

4. Plant
True leaves unfold and make food. The plant uses the food to grow more leaves, roots, flowers and fruit.

3. Growing up
Two tiny seed leaves hidden inside the seed act like a packed lunch. They give the plant the energy it needs to grow up and out of the earth.

Seed leaf

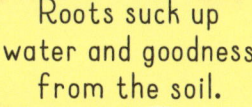
Hello world!

Roots suck up water and goodness from the soil.

19

Drinking Water

Plants drink water, just like us! They suck it up from the soil using their roots. Water travels upwards, through tiny bundles of tubes in the stem and it floats into the air from holes in the leaves!

2. Drink up
Water travels up the stem through tubes called xylem.

3. Spread out
Water travels into every leaf through tubes called veins.

1. Wet soil
Rain soaks into the soil. It breaks down rocks and mixes with things like rotting leaves and insect poo. All this goodness gets drunk by the plant!

Making Food

Imagine you didn't need to eat breakfast and instead you could lie in the sun and food would magically appear inside your belly! It sounds ridiculous, but it happens inside plants. It's called photosynthesis. That's a big long word but if we break it down, 'photo' means 'light' and 'synthesis' means 'to put together'. So a plant puts together food using light!

Ingredients
- **Water:** from the soil
- **Carbon dioxide gas:** from the air
- **A pinch of salt:** from the soil
- **Sunshine**

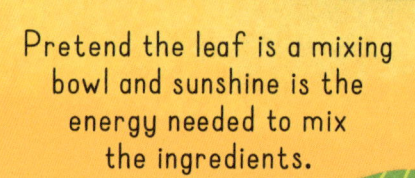

Pretend the leaf is a mixing bowl and sunshine is the energy needed to mix the ingredients.

Sunshine makes the ingredients change into something new – a sugar and some waste gas. The sugar is food for the plant.

The food made in the leaves is a sugary juice. It travels round the plant through tubes.

Did you know...?
Tiny green parts in leaves called chloroplasts are where food gets made during photosynthesis.

CO_2

O_2

When juicy food from the leaves reaches the roots they grow a little longer.

Thank you, plants!

When the leaf makes food there are some leftovers that the plant chucks out. The leftovers are a gas called oxygen. It floats away out of the leaves.

We need the oxygen gas that is chucked out by leaves during photosynthesis. It's the gas we breathe in! So next time you take a breath, remember to thank plants!

Organising Plants

There are more than 400,000 different kinds of plants. We call each kind a species. And in each species, there are different colours and shapes. We call those varieties. Scientists like to name things and put them into groups. One way they do this is by putting together plants that flower and those that don't.

Non-flowering plants include moss, ferns and pine trees. These ancient plants have been around since the time of the dinosaurs!

Most non-flowering plants grow baby plants by spreading spores. Spores are so small they blow away in the wind.

Ferns grow spores on the underside of their curly leaves called fronds.

Non-flowering trees called conifers have hard woody shapes called cones instead of flowers. Cones contain pollen.

When pollen blows from a boy cone into a girl cone, the girl cone can make seeds.

Did you know...?
Fungi aren't plants. They don't make food using photosynthesis and they are more closely related to animals than plants!

Flowering Plants

Most plants make flowers. Do you remember the tiny little leaves that are hidden inside seeds? They store energy like a packed lunch. Well, some flowering plants have one seed leaf and some have two. We call the one-seed-leaf sort monocots, and the two-leaf sorts dicots.

In the monocots group we have the grass family. It includes bamboo, wheat and sugar cane.

A family is a group of plants that are related to each other.

Another family of monocots is palms!

Then there's the orchid family, with over 28,000 species.

In the dicots group there are even more flower families.

The pea family has over 20,000 different trees, vines, herbs and shrubs. It includes peanuts, lentils, soya beans and, of course, peas.

The rose family isn't just roses. It's raspberries, almonds, apples, cherries, pears, plumbs, mountain ash and many more species.

Sunflowers, dandelions, thistles, lettuce, and many others, including daisies, are part of the daisy family.

Daisy family flowers are made of lots of tiny flowers clumped together in a floret. If you pull out a petal you'll discover it's actually a very tiny complete flower – wow!

Grasses

When you think of grass you might think of a green lawn or a football pitch. But there's much more to grass than that! Grasses are actually one of the most important plant families on Earth – because they feed us.

One important grass is wheat. Grass fruit is called grain. We grind grain to make flour – perfect for cooking bread or pasta!

Rice is a grass that grows in warm, wet areas. We boil the grain and eat it.

Sugar cane is a grass we crush and boil to make sugar. If you like sweets, you can thank grass!

Trees & the Seasons

Trees are big beautiful plants with thick, woody stems and strong roots. They don't stop growing after a few years, like we do. Instead they keep growing taller and wider over their whole lives. They also change throughout the year in a pattern with the seasons. This is how a horse chestnut changes through the year...

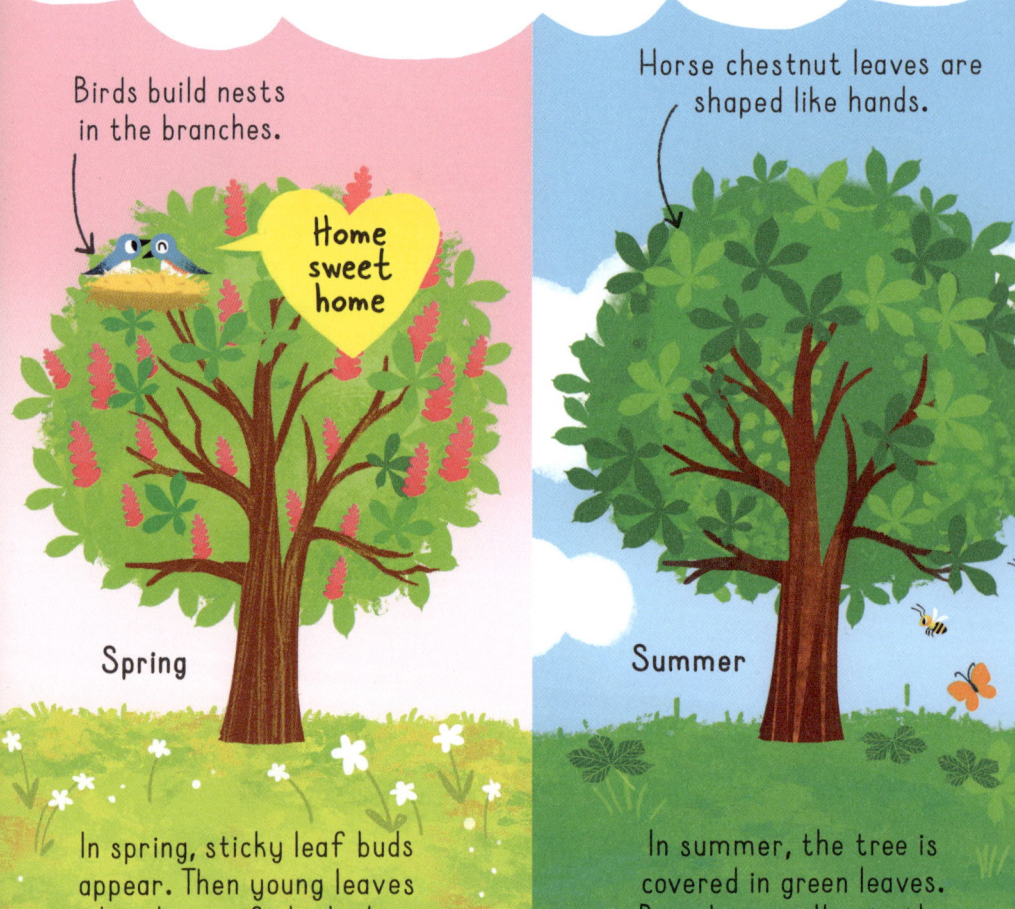

Birds build nests in the branches.

Home sweet home

Spring

Horse chestnut leaves are shaped like hands.

Summer

In spring, sticky leaf buds appear. Then young leaves break out of the buds. The leaves make food. After that, pink and white flowers bloom.

In summer, the tree is covered in green leaves. Bees bring pollen to the flowers. After this, the flowers begin to turn into fruit.

Did you know...?
A tree trunk is protected by bark. Just like our skin, bark is a waterproof layer that keeps germs out. Bark is a dead layer so it flakes off as new bark grows below. Your skin does the same!

The tree's fruit ripens and drops off. Inside is a shiny conker.

Autumn

Winter

In autumn, the tree gets ready for winter. It moves food stored in its leaves back into the trunk and down into its roots. This makes the leaves turn yellow, red and brown and they fall off.

The tree looks naked without its leaves. It uses food stored in its roots to keep growing through the winter.

Types of Tree

There are two main groups we put trees into. Deciduous trees lose their leaves every year, just like the horse chestnut. Then there are trees that keep green leaves all year round. We call them evergreens. Trees have invented ways to survive in the places where they live.

Conifers live in cold, snowy places. Snow slips easily off their thin evergreen leaves called needles.

During tropical storms, coconut trees bend over and spring back. Strong roots anchor the tree, and gaps between leaves let the wind through.

The lombi tree has huge roots that spread out above ground because the soil is shallow. That way, the tree doesn't fall over.

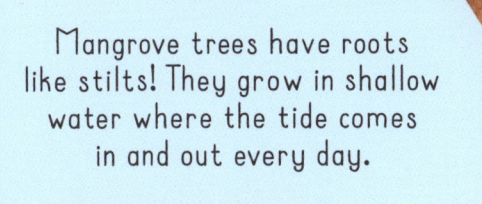

Mangrove trees have roots like stilts! They grow in shallow water where the tide comes in and out every day.

Mangrove forests are a natural barrier against giant waves called tsunamis.

These trees don't drown because they keep part of their roots above the water. They can filter the salt out of seawater before they drink it, too.

A tree grows a new layer on the outside of its trunk every year.

This slice through the trunk shows the layers. You can count these growth rings to see how old it is.

Resin oozes from a tree if its bark is damaged. It sets to heal the wound, like a scab.

Leaves

Leaves come in all different shapes and sizes. Each type of plant has its own leaf shape. They can be heart-shaped or cloud-shaped or star-shaped or shaped like an arrow.

The patterns on the edges of the leaf help us to know which plant it is.

Did you know...?
Sometimes you can see the veins that carry water around the leaf.

A waxy coating called resin stops the water in pine needles from freezing in winter.

Water lilies have big round leaves with air bubbles inside them – this makes them float on water.

Bulbs are underground leaves that store energy over winter, ready for new plants to grow.

Defence

Plants work hard to make flowers and fruit and to spread their seeds. Some have invented ways to protect themselves so that they can stay alive!

Thorns are branches with sharp tips. Spines are super spiky leaves or parts of leaves.

Giraffes have leathery tongues so they can eat prickly plants without getting hurt.

A cactus has spines for protection. Spines lose less water than leaves – that's useful if you live in a hot, dry desert!

Plant Attack

Some plants can trap and eat insects! These fascinating plants are called carnivorous plants. A carnivore is a name for a meat eater. Then there are plants that attach themselves to other plants and steal their water. They are called parasitic plants.

The strangler fig grows by wrapping itself around the outside of a tree. It steals water from the tree and eventually, the tree beneath is completely covered up so it can't get light or air.

Mistletoe berries are so sticky that when birds eat them, they need to wipe their beaks clean on tree branches. The mistletoe grows on the branch it gets wiped off onto.

The pitcher plant lures insects in with its sweet nectar. Insects slip into the plant's liquid, get dissolved... and then eaten.

Some rainforest pitcher plants even eat small rodents!

Bladderworts live partly in water. They use a suction pouch to suck in passing insects!

The Venus fly trap has leaves that snap shut when tiny hairs detect an insect walking over them.

Sundews have hairs with sticky blobs on the end of them. They work like glue, sticking to visiting insects.

Weird & Wonderful

Plants can be super strange... and super awesome! Here are some more of the biggest, smelliest, weirdest and most wonderful plants on the planet.

The bee orchid looks and smells like a girl bee. A boy bee visits it to try to get a girlfriend.

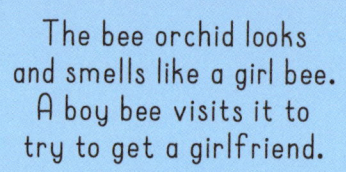

Oh, hello!

The tallest trees are redwoods.

They can grow over 100 metres tall.

The spiky sweet thorn tree can survive forest fires, drought and frost. Small shoots grow up from the roots if the tree is burnt down.

A big underground root called a taproot stores food for the thorn tree for when it is cold.

Ant plants let ants live inside them. The ants have a home and they help the plant by eating up invading insects. The plant drinks ant poo and gets goodness from it.

The durian and ginkgo plants smell like sick! They may smell bad on the outside, but they taste sweet inside. Insects love their pongy smell.

The bristlecone pine tree can live to 5,000 years old!

The rafflesia plant has the biggest flower on the planet. It's over a metre wide. It's also known as the corpse lily because it stinks of rotting meat!

41

Thank you, Plants!

Plants are amazing! We make them into food and fuel and so many other useful things. We use them to make medicine and they clean our air. If you're reading this book on paper, it's made from a tree! Plants really help us, but how can we help them?

One way to help plants is to help insects. You can make homes for bees out of tubes or log piles.

The more bees we have, the more flowers can get pollinated, leading to even more plants!

You could plant wild flowers in your garden, school or street to feed bees.

Two in five plant species are in danger of dying out forever, all because of us humans. Plants really do need our help!

You can tell everyone how important plants are. Ask adults to plant trees, to make up for all those that humans have chopped down.

If you draw pictures of plants and look carefully at their different parts, it helps you to notice them and feel grateful for them.

Scientists name about 2,000 new plants every year. Maybe one day, you will find a plant that's never been spotted by a scientist before. You can give it a name and make sure it stays protected forever!

Glossary

Family
A group of different species that are related to one another. For example, the rose family includes almonds and cherry trees.

Fruit
The part of a plant with seeds in it. This is often brightly coloured and tasty to animals.

Fungi
Fungi stay still and grow but are not plants or animals. Fungi do not photosynthesise. A mushroom is a type of fungus. So is mould.

Leaves
The parts of plants that catch sunlight and make food during photosynthesis. Leaves are often green, and can be all different shapes and sizes.

Nectar
A sweet, sugary juice made in flowers to attract pollinators.

Ovary
A hollow place inside a flower. Seeds grow inside it.

Oxygen
A gas made by plants. All living things need it to survive. We breathe oxygen in from the air.

Petal
The outer part of a flower, often colourful to attract insects.

Photosynthesis
The way plants make food in leaves. They mix carbon dioxide gas (from the air) with water (from the soil) and they use sunlight to make a sugar.

Poison
Something that is dangerous or deadly if swallowed.

Pollen
A powder made inside flowers. It makes seeds grow when it reaches an ovary.

Pollinators
Living things that carry pollen between flowers. They include bees, wasps, flies, moths, bats and birds.

Roots
Underground parts of a plant that take goodness and water in from the soil. Roots help the plant to stay up and in one place.

Seed
The part of a plant that makes baby plants when it is planted in the right conditions.

Soil
The top layer of brown earth that plants grow in. It is made from broken up rock and dead things that have rotted away. Soil has water and goodness trapped inside it.

Species
A kind of plant, for example a rose.

Stem
The part of a plant that grows upwards from the seed. Buds, leaves, flowers and branches grow out from it.

Variety
A different coloured or shaped plant from one species, for example different coloured roses.